Then *I* Met the Master

12 Great Songs

BY GOSPEL MUSIC HALL OF FAME SONGWRITER

Mosie Lister

ARRANGED FOR CHOIR BY RICHARD KINGSMORE

978.083.4170.70⁴

Lillenas PUBLISHING COMPANY
KANSAS CITY, MO 64141

Contents

Then I Met the Master

Words and Music by
MOSIE LISTER
Arranged by Richard Kingsmore

CD: 3

I am one of His own. For
all things were changed when He found me; A
new day broke through all a-round me; For

12

You Are My Song

Words and Music by
MOSIE LISTER
Arranged by Richard Kingsmore

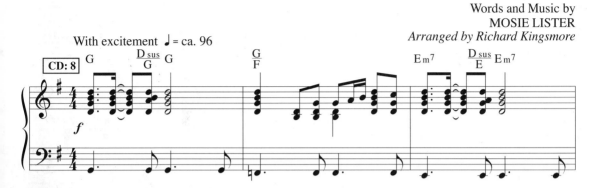

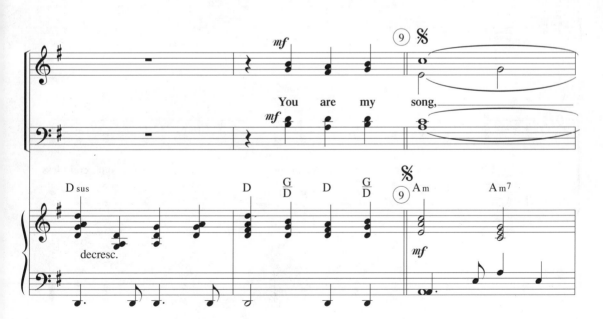

You are my song,

15

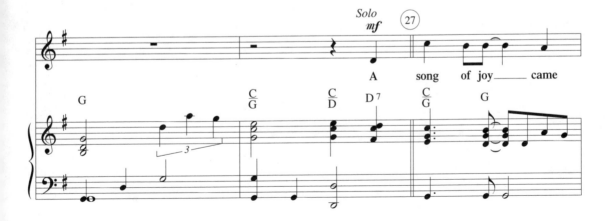

in - to my heart one morn - ing;_____ My

world came a - live when I heard the mel - o - dy._____

Duet

The Sun broke thro',____ and a brand new day____ came

CD: 12

I Won't Turn Back

Words and Music by
MOSIE LISTER
Arranged by Richard Kingsmore

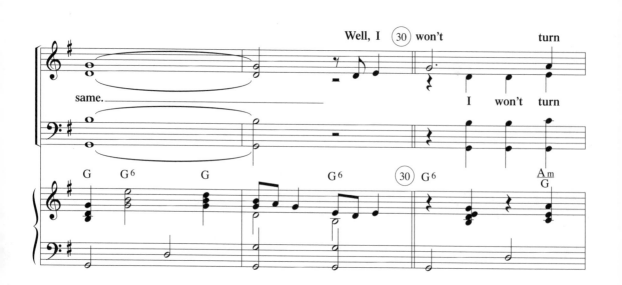

26

29

Where No One Stands Alone

Words and Music by
MOSIE LISTER
Arranged by Richard Kingsmore

hand; let me stand Where

no one stands a - lone.

Hold my

Where no one stands a - lone. Hold my

46

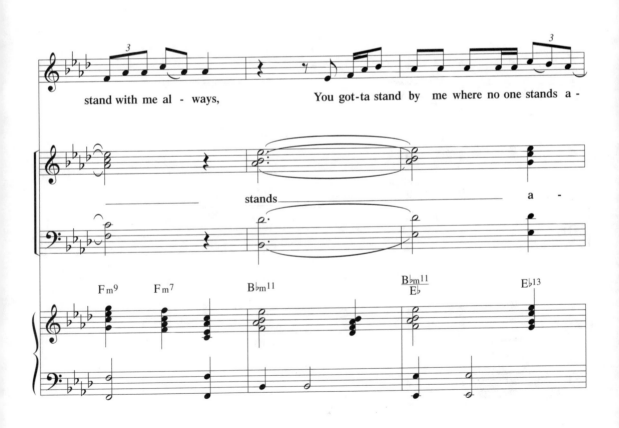

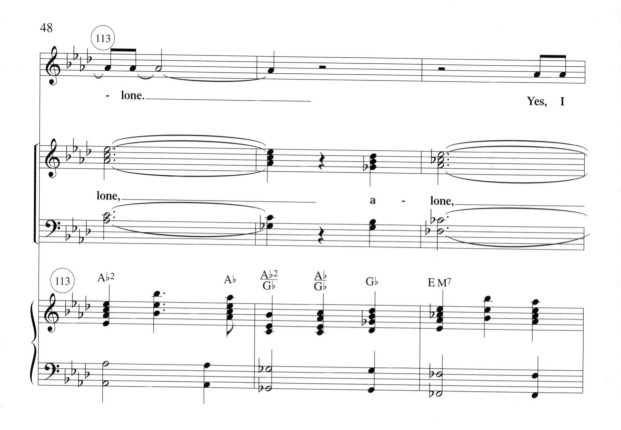

Let Some Drops Fall on Me

with

There Shall Be Showers of Blessing

Words and Music by
MOSIE LISTER
Arranged by Richard Kingsmore

52

*"There Shall Be Showers of Blessing"

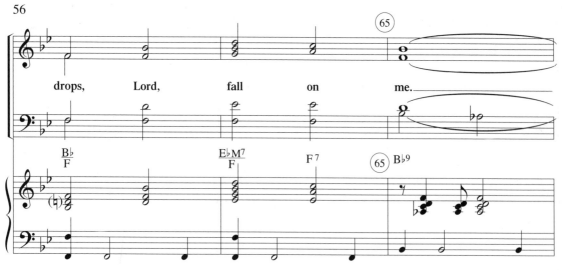

drops,   Lord,   fall   on   me.

CD: 33

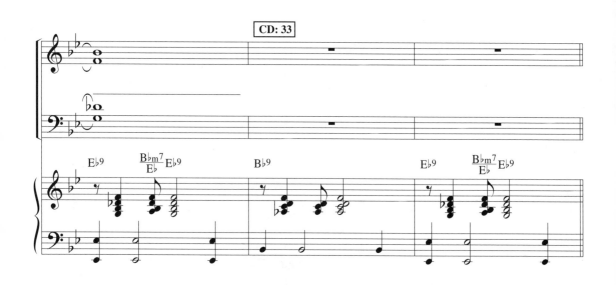

Basses only

Bless me, Je - sus,   Let   the   show - ers fall.

Bless me, Je - sus, Let the show - ers fall,

Let some drops, Lord, fall on

me!

Holy Lamb of God

Words and Music by
MOSIE LISTER
Arranged by Richard Kingsmore

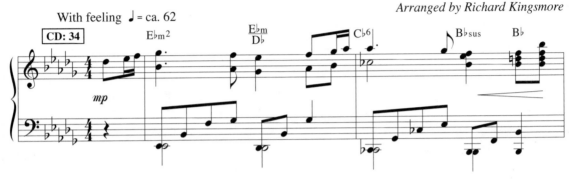

In this ho - ly place we bow to - day and

Higher on the Mountain

Words and Music by
MOSIE LISTER
Arranged by Richard Kingsmore

on the bless-ed mount of ev-er-last-ing love.

moun - tain of His love.

A   D7   G   C/G   G   29 C

CD: 41

Unison

I see the

G D/F# Em Cm6/Eb G/D Am/D Bm/D D7 G G/F Eb7

lights   on   the moun-tain,   shin - ing ev - er bright-er.   They're

Do,   do,   do,   do,

Unison

33 Ab   Ab7   Db   Db° Db

74

One of Your Children Needs You, Lord

Words and Music by
MOSIE LISTER
Arranged by Richard Kingsmore

PLEASE NOTE: Copying of this product is not covered by CCLI licenses. For CCLI information call 1-800-234-2446.

needs You, Lord. One of Your chil - dren

needs You, Lord. Je - sus, Je - sus, be

near. Je - sus,

Take Me to the Fountain

with
Nothing but the Blood

Words and Music by
MOSIE LISTER
Arranged by Richard Kingsmore

Noth - in' but the___

nev - er shall run dry.___

F/C   C7   Db7sus   Db7

52 *"Nothing but the Blood"

blood.

O   pre - cious   is   the   flow___

52   Gb   Db/F   Gb

to the liv - ing foun - tain._____ Nev - er

To the liv - ing foun - tain that nev - er

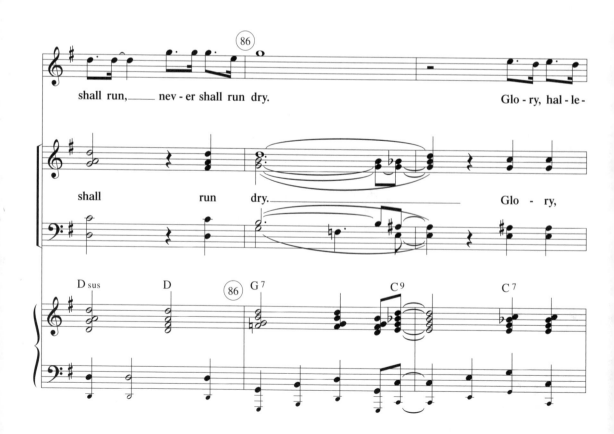

shall run,___ nev - er shall run dry. Glo - ry, hal - le -

shall run dry.___ Glo - ry,

Call Home

Words and Music by
MOSIE LISTER
Arranged by Richard Kingsmore

Ladies unison

There is a mo - ment

While Ages Roll

with

O That Will Be Glory

Words and Music by
MOSIE LISTER
Arranged by Richard Kingsmore

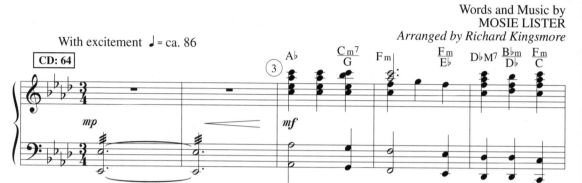

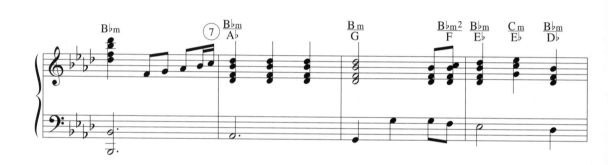

When They Call My Name

Words and Music by
MOSIE LISTER
Arranged by Richard Kingsmore

call - ing my name,_____ Calling me yon - der to that

call - ing my name,_____ They'll call me to that

C7   F7

Heav - en - ly plain,_____ And when I see them swing - ing wide those

Heav - en - ly plain,_____ And when they swing those

F7   17   Bb7

pearl - y gates,_____ I'll be read - y, I won't have to

pearl - y gates,_____

Bb7   Cb7   Bb7   Eb6

132

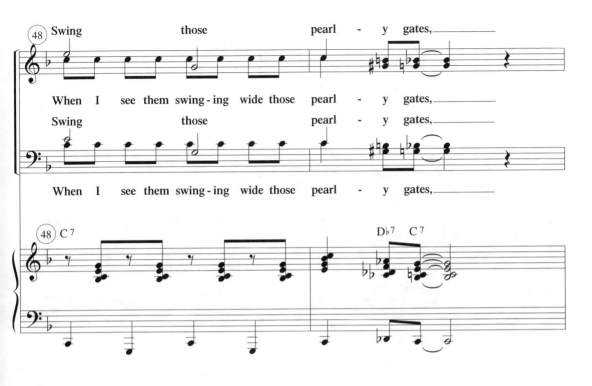

134

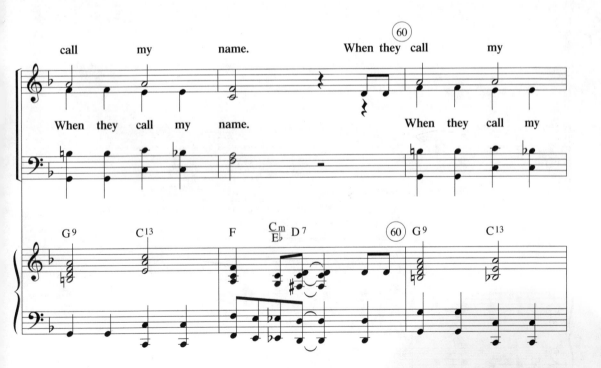

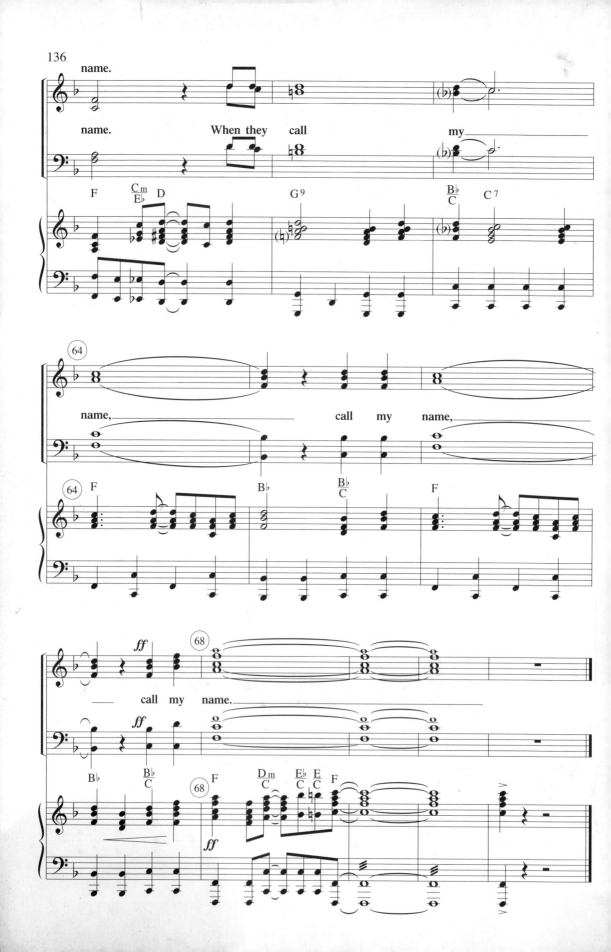